THE TYNE STRANGLER – MARY BELL NEWCASTLES 11 YEAR OLD CHILD KILLER

By Stu Armstrong

ISBN: 9798866920006

Copyright © 2023 Stu Armstrong

All rights reserved.

No part of this book may be copied or reproduced in any way shape or form without the express permission of the Author.

Table of Contents

PROLOGUE 3
CHAPTER ONE 5
   SCOTSWOOD, NEWCASTLE 5
CHAPTER TWO 9
   THE BELL FAMILY 9
CHAPTER THREE 11
   VIOLENT TENDENCIES 11
CHAPTER FOUR 16
   FEAR 16
CHAPTER FIVE 18
   MARTIN BROWN 18
Chapter Six 25
   Summer in Scottswood 25
CHAPTER SEVEN 27
   BRIAN HOWE 27
CHAPTER EIGHT 32

PRIME SUSPECT	32
CHAPTER NINE	*35*
ARRESTS MADE	35
CHAPTER TEN	*39*
EVIDENCE	39
CHAPTER ELEVEN	*43*
THE TRIAL BEGINS	43
CHAPTER TWELVE	*58*
WHY?	58
CHAPTER THIRTEEN	*65*
FUTURE	65

PROLOGUE

Mary would massage the boys' necks and tell them that they had a sore throat and not to worry she would make it better, then her hands would tighten………….

In 1968 an 11-year-old girl Mary Bell killed two little boys in the Scotswood area of the West End of Newcastle.

The killings caused bewilderment and outrage the people of Newcastle were horrified by the killing of two defenceless toddlers.

It was almost too much for

people in the area, known to be a very caring city, to try and come to terms with this.

CHAPTER ONE

SCOTSWOOD, NEWCASTLE

Scotswood, where Mary Bell grew up in the 1960s had barely changed since the war, it was a slum area with all the social problems that come with years of neglect and deprivation. There were a lot of notorious families in the area who were well known to the police for drunkenness minor petty crime and that sort of thing a lot of pubs in that area a legacy from the days of the factory the heavy industrial area and it was common for husbands to be drunk and calls to the police were very frequent to respond to fights in the houses and in the streets.

Mary lived in a generally bad area, almost every other house had a prostitute of some sort, and it shows she shared that kind of environment growing up.

It's a hard life for people who have to live in this constant battle trying to
determine who was in the right and who wasn't.

In the back-to-back housing estates of Scotswood, children like Mary were left to play unsupervised for hours in the streets, it was a time of growing prosperity in Britain but this newfound wealth never quite made its way to Newcastle's West End with many living in abject poverty, the mums used to keep the coal in the kitchens because they wouldn't put in the bunker outside in case it was stolen, they wouldn't hang washing anything outside in case it was stolen, the vast majority of houses that didn't have much but they just used to get on with it.

Newcastle was in the grip of massive redevelopment, slums were being knocked down to make way for new high-rise flats and the demolition sites of Scotswood 'Rat Alley' would become a children's playground, as the city changed by the day.

For all of its faults and they were legion, Scotswood, like most of Newcastle was well known to be a friendly place, nobody had anything so it was all community spirit.

CHAPTER TWO

THE BELL FAMILY

Betty had quite a reputation in the area, she was a Brass a lady of ill repute, a prostitute.

They were a difficult family and Mary's childhood had been full of unhappiness she was neglected both her parents were often away the family lived in the White House Rd it was the roughest part
of the area.

Betty was depressive and erratic, on one occasion she tried to have Mary adopted yet on another she rejected her family's offers to take her daughter off her hands.

Betty had a reputation in the area
the whole estate knew about Mary's mum, she would just go away for sometimes for weeks on end working as a prostitute.

Mary spent much time on her own in the house when her mother was out with clients. Billy her father was a petty criminal and a drunk, Mary's father was well known to the police he was a big rough bloke a muscular type of man, not the kind of man one would have liked to meet on a dark night.

CHAPTER THREE

VIOLENT TENDENCIES

When one considers that Mary was brought up in a household like that this could she possibly have become disturbed mentally?

Her behaviour was well known in the playground, playing for one minute and doing the things normal kids do and then she would start upsetting the other kids and that's when the change would start, she would become aggressive.

One 9-year-old who was in School with Mary commented *"I can remember I was frightened so I kept away from her, but she would come to me and say Oh who are you, your playing, turn your back and her eyes change and she would act funny and would shake and then would show how she could get you by the throat at least once she did it to a younger girl at school and held her hand around her throat so tight that her eyes bulged and her face was red, she went a different colour when Mary was choking her, but my sister who was bigger made sure she got her off"*

Teachers at Delaval Road also became aware that she seemed to have a sadistic streak, someone in the class came in one morning and had her mark on her cheek and I asked about what it was she said that Mary had stepped out a cigarette on her cheek and eyes.

Marys's violent behaviour was noticed by her teachers but tragically nothing was done to address her problems and at home, she was exposed to the grim world of her mother's prostitution and her father's drunkenness.

Mary was influenced by all of these things she saw very strange behaviour going on through her own mother's actions by her father's actions and by the local community she was deeply embedded in a sort of petty crime environment an environment in which violence against each other was something that was almost acceptable and the norm next door to Mary in White House Rd, lived another girl called Bell who is no relation, she was Norma Bell two years older than Mary but much less bright.

Mary was always the leader because she had some followers which led her to do things that maybe she wouldn't have done on her own. She could dominate people quite easily if Mary were to tell Norma to jump off the Tyne Bridge, then she would jump off the Tyne Bridge.

CHAPTER FOUR

FEAR

The children of Scotswood had come to fear Mary & Norma and for some reason. On Saturday the 11th of May 1968 Mary & Norma had picked up a boy aged three years old and taken him to buy some sweets, sometime later he was found wandering dazed and bleeding the police and an ambulance were called but no action was taken.

The next day the mother of a

local girl complained to the police that Mary had attempted to strangle her daughter who was playing in the sandpit, but once more despite all the signs nothing was done to take Mary in hand.

Norma and Mary had grabbed her by the neck and started to strangle her, she managed somehow to break free and jumped up and managed to evade a struggle and get free and run home, Action yet again wasn't taken, little Pauline had not told the full story as was terrified.

CHAPTER FIVE

MARTIN BROWN

Saturday the 25th of May, Martin Brown a four-year-old Scotswood boy was playing outside with his friends he was quite tall for his age and well-built with blonde curly hair blue eyes and a cheeky face was mischievous like when he decided they had a swimming pool in the bedroom when he filled a bottom draw full of water, his room ended up flooded.

It wasn't unusual for children to be out late playing in the derelict buildings of 'rat alley', so Martins family weren't concerned at first by his long absence but at 5 pm a neighbour called to say that he had had an accident, the family

Ran up to the houses and a centre crowd of people stood outside and this man had Martin in his hands he was grey, and he felt cold and this man has tears running down his face.

They asked if he was alright, and man mam simply replied I don't know,
and at that two ambulance men just rushed past grabbed him and put him into the ambulance.

Martin Brown was taken from the derelict house to the local hospital in Newcastle and pronounced dead on arrival. There was not a mark on him apart from a little trickle of blood down his face.

Because Martin's body had been found in mysterious circumstances upstairs inside an abandoned house the police were called in to investigate the cause of death.

At first, the thoughts were that maybe he had taken some tablets because some tablets were lying around but that wasn't the case, and they were left by the previous tenant of the house. The pathologist carried out an extensive examination of the boy's throat but couldn't conclude if it was a violent or a
natural death.
Two days later Monday the 27th of May police were called to a Scotswood nursery, close to Mary and Norma Bell's homes where there had been a break-in.

Police officers found four pieces of paper, scribbled on one were the words *"I murder so that I may come back"* and another *"We murder watch out"* and on another "We did murder Martin brown fuck off"

At the time the notes were dismissed by the police as a nasty childish game, the general feel of these notes was to tease and provoke the police because of their lack of progress.

Norma presented as a very pathetic child and Mary dominated her that same Monday Mary Bell went to school as usual and wrote in her school newsbook there were crowds of people beside an old house and she asked what was the matter there and had been told that a boy had just laid down and died!

She had also drawn a picture of the dead body of Martin brown, and next to it a bottle by which she wrote tablets, Mary
also showed a workman finding the body.

Just before Martin was buried Mary and Norma knocked on his mother's door and asked if they could come into the house and see Martin, they knew he was dead and asked to come in and see him in his coffin.

Chapter Six

Summer in Scottswood

Two months passed that summer in Newcastle without incident, but the case of Martin brown was not forgotten, without a known cause, his death was blamed on the dangerous conditions in the slums in Newcastle that were derelict.

The locals reacted to this situation in perhaps the traditional ways of shock and horror. The murder occurred in in a part of the city which was being demolished for slum clearance, and the local population marched to complain that this was not being done properly and effectively, During the protest, at the front was a strange little thing, carrying one of the banners was, this was Mary bell

CHAPTER SEVEN

BRIAN HOWE

There was a young killer at large who despite all the signs was not apprehended. Tragically another death was inevitable and on Wednesday the 31st of July.

Brian Howe a 3-year-old was like so many children in Scotswood playing unsupervised in the streets.

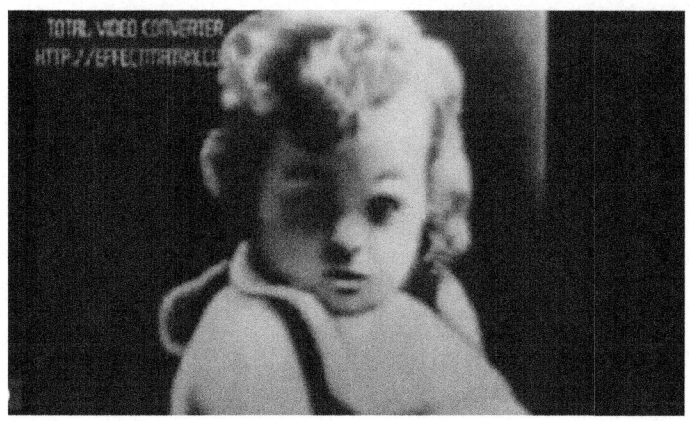

He went to watch the demolition of derelict houses in Rat Alley and then a little later Mary Bell picked him up and took him off with Norma to play on a nearby patch of waste ground, called 'The Tin Lizzy', he was never seen alive again.

His family knew that he had gone missing but didn't connect it with Mary Bell. Late at night, the police descended on the waste ground, complete with floodlights lighting up the area where they found the body of the murdered 3-year-old.

The area was cordoned off and the police examined the body of a little boy with blonde curly hair.He appeared to be dead, and the doctor and a crime scene photographer were called to the scene.

The boy was found lying semi-spread eagle and half naked amongst the concrete and Bush's.It was noticed that there had been snippets of the boy's hair cut off and lying nearby, and his legs showed that there were puncture wounds in the calves of the legs and other areas of the legs.

This seemed to indicate that perhaps the scissors or whatever implement had been used to cut the boy's hair had also been used to puncture his legs.

Straight away the post-mortem showed that Brian Howe had been strangled and that the cut marks were naive attempts to carve initials on the body of the young child.

The also pathologist concluded it was the work of a child. The similarities with the death of little Martin Brown made police re-open their investigation.

CHAPTER EIGHT

PRIME SUSPECT

To the horror of the local community, the police announced that they were searching for a double child killer and amid the hundreds of suspects one child stood out to police, Mary Bell.

It was almost like she seemed to want to draw attention to herself, whenever police held a meeting or press conference this one girl's face kept appearing listening intently to everything that was being said and always pushing herself forward. Police couldn't miss her if they tried.

It was common knowledge to the local children that Mary and Norma Bell had been up to no good Mary had already boasted in the playground that she had strangled someone, it was thought that everybody who went to the same school knew what she was like.

Police decided it was time to have a word with Mary Bell and they visited the house. When they knocked on the door Mr bell, the father, refused to let them see the young girl, and he held back a very large aggressive Alsatian dog which he threatened to set on the police.

But, little did many people know, there had been a witness. A 9-year-old boy with a mental age of 4 had seen everything and explained to police what had gone on and it appears that Mary's method was to massage the neck of the boys and tell them that they have sore throats and that she could make it better, and then her grip tightened and tightened until they died

Given the new witness officers were ordered to go down to Scotswood and bring Mary and Norma in for questioning, the police consulted a child psychiatrist to get advice on how best to treat their children.

CHAPTER NINE

ARRESTS MADE

This was now more than just suspicions, also the school told police that they had suspicions because they behaved curiously in the school. It was difficult to get Mary relaxed, she knew she was suspected.

When the police went to her house she sat and matter of factly said *"Send for my solicitor"*

She was tough for a child, right from the very beginning, all the way to the end of the trial.
It was a constant denial on Mary's part, although she had other things on her mind as well for instance, she would wonder about her mother and if she was going to come to see her or where her mother was, she had an Alsatian dog, and she would ask about that.

When getting off the subject of the death of the little boy, she began to talk about her friendship with Norma and how they had been happy together and were full of laughter on the day that this child died.

In the evenings Mary and her friend Norma were taken into care in Newcastle, and many of those who came into contact with Mary grew fond of this vivacious and intelligent girl who was in such trouble.

She was only 11 years of age she didn't realise the enormity of her predicament she didn't realise what she was facing in her future life.

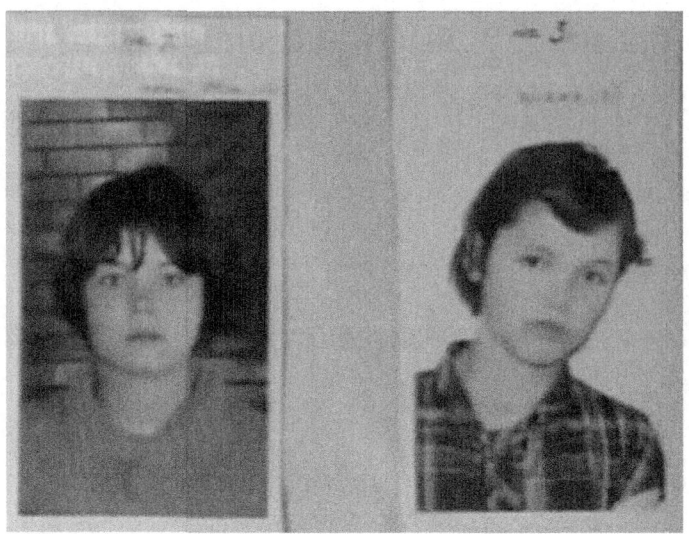

At Westgate Road police station, where she was interviewed, Mary astonished the police with the sophisticated way in which she answered their questions, almost as if she was a computer, when starting to ask a question she was not only answering almost before the question was finished but then should continue and answer the next four or five questions still unasked.

CHAPTER TEN

EVIDENCE

Despite her denials the evidence against Mary began to mount up the scissors used to mark the body of Brian which were found near the scene and the police now made the connection between Mary and the notes they had found after Martin Brown's death.

Two months previously more evidence came from the girl's School, Eric Foster, Mary Bell's

teacher who had always been fond of the intelligent little
girl in his class told police that after he learned of her arrest, he decided to go back over her school books to check if she had written anything about the deaths of the two boys.

She had extraordinarily written on the cover a headline 'Boy found dead in old house' the report was written inside.

This had been written on the Monday after the weekend that the boy had died, all about how this little boy had gone into these houses and just lay down and died, and when the police looked at the book and they saw the drawing at the bottom there were there was the tablets arrowed police said that was never disclosed to anyone so she must have been there to have seen it

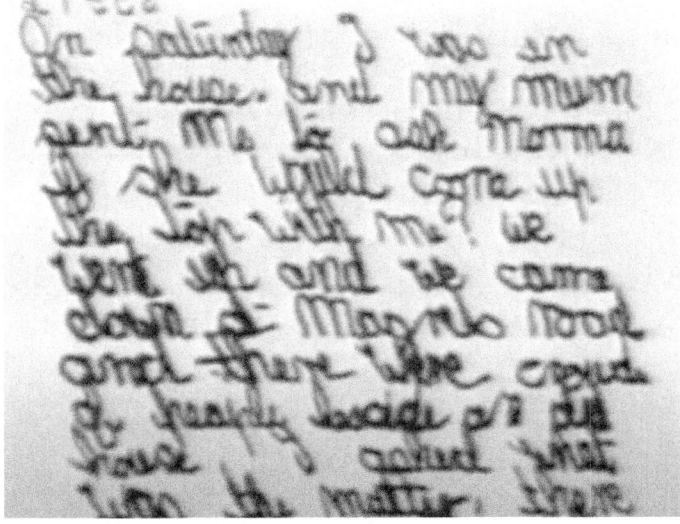

The school book was proof that she had been involved and on the 8th of August 1968, the police charged Mary Bell and her friend Norma Bell with the murder of Brian Howell.

CHAPTER ELEVEN

THE TRIAL BEGINS

Four months later on the 5th of December, the full trial of Mary and Norma began that Newcastle Assizes, although the case had many similarities with the murder of James Bulger 25 years later there was none of the sensational reporting that would be expected today.

Indeed, because it involved a child killer the BBC and ITN banned the story from their daytime News bulletins.

Both Mary and Norma claimed they were innocent and blamed each other for the killings, and as with the Bulger case later many felt a Crown Court the wrong place for the law to deal with children

It was thought that it had to go through the normal criminal processes and appear in an open court, along with all of the paraphernalia of counsel for the defence and counsel for the prosecution and the like, the whole thing focused on these two tiny little figures with dark hair and big dark eyes looking out into the world from the dock.

This wasn't really suitable for examining the truths in this situation and the children were unable to properly respond to this situation there was no chance of it being a fair just trial but some effort was made to ease the situation of the little girls the trial judge set the scene by deciding that the lawyers representing Mary and anybody else should sit with the client and therefore remove some of the impersonal feel that they might otherwise have been, and even that which may seem quite a small thing concerning the whole trial procedure helped because Mary was able to speak to her council whenever she wanted, and they could speak to her whenever wanted.

There's no question of dealing at arm's length and the jury would be aware of that more relaxed atmosphere as well.

Seeing her sitting there one would wonder how on earth she could be involved in any crime she looked innocent, but she showed no emotion and gave her answers straightforwardly and constantly maintained that she was not guilty of either of the killings.

There was an incident when she was being cross-examined when she became very upset, she was asked whether she had actually killed a pigeon by strangulation and that upset her greatly a break had to be called while she recovered from this.

Tears in court as girls are accused of boy's murder

By Journal Reporter

THE YOUNGER of two girls jointly accused of murdering a three-year-old boy, wept at the end of the eight-minute hearing before Newcastle magistrates yesterday.

The girls, aged 11 and 13, were remanded in custody for a week, when they will appear on remand before the juvenile court. They are accused of the

Judge halts hearing as accused girls weep

Girls used razor blade to cut initials on dead boy—Q.C.

Child 'has abnormal urge'
Q.C. tells of three throat-squeezing attacks by girl

Judge's plea to women jurors

Jury told of 'coffin' incident

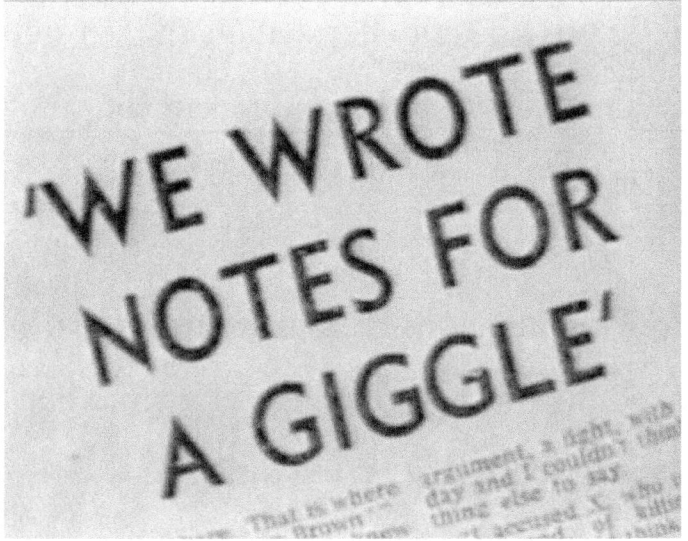

Girls laughed over Martin's death—witness

'WE WROTE NOTES FOR A GIGGLE'

The two girls Were very different in personality, Mary was bright and sharp and could answer back to the council when they questioned her, she could make quite witty little remarks the other girl was not as bright, and was completely overawed by the setting and less sense, the court almost separated the two and said therefore the bright one must have done it and the duller one probably didn't there is no doubt in the court given all the evidence that Mary had strangled the two little boys despite her denials the verdict of the jury dependent on the findings of the psychiatrists who examined Mary

The doctors' conclusions were unanimous that Mary lacked the ordinary feelings of a child her age and was in their view at the time she was a psychopath.

Norma: 'She is an insecure little girl'

The Scotswood murder trial: fifth day

Mary is a dangerous psychopath, say doctors

The Scotswood murder trial: sixth day

One of the doctors commented

"I did not get any feeling of sadness from behind the glass you see most children you will get to know, and they talk, and you get a feeling about what sort of a child they are, in my particular job you have to, but I don't think that was one where you could do this" And another commented *"Oh well she was an intelligent child, she got it all worked out, she was devious and that that's very often characteristic of a psychopath is that they have considerable intelligence and resource and cunning and she used those to the full"*

Given the medical diagnosis, Mary Bell was found guilty Bell was acquitted because she was simple-minded and had been dominated by her friend she left the court and returned to her home and family in Scotswood.

Mary was sentenced to be detained at Her Majesty's pleasure, Mary was in a state then of very great shock and understandably so, she broke down in tears and her barrister sitting next to her put his arm around her in an attempt to comfort her.

Being found guilty not of a charge of murder but guilty of manslaughter the authority's duty was to rehabilitate and not to punish Mary Bell.

Even the newspapers agreed, and even The Sun in contrast to his attitude to the Bulger case 25 years later called for a humane and caring approach to the little girl killer but the problem was the case at that time was unique she was too young to be the subject of a hospital order under the Mental Health Act that wasn't an option.

One of the strange features of this trial was that after she had been convicted it was apparent that nobody had even thought where she was going to spend the first night, or what to do with her. Eventually, it was decided that she should go to an approved school with secure accommodation, Redbank in Lancashire. Mary would be looked after and given the attention and even love she craved and lacked at home.

Her Barrister stated *"Mary was and I believe still is a very attractive personality of a lively mind and with quite a lot of gifts in the artistic field and the capacity to write well and relate well which was really quite remarkable coming from the the background that she did do and I think that all sorts of people professionals and lawyers and others involved in her care were quite taken by this this innocence was very fortunate because what it did mean is that nobody was prepared just to let her case lie fallow"*

After the dust had settled those involved reflected on what had caused a Newcastle girl only just 11 to kill two boys in her neighbourhood there was little desire for retribution and much for understanding.

CHAPTER TWELVE

WHY?

Most blamed mirror behaviour on her environment and the fact that her mother was a prostitute, in the haunted eyes of Mary Bell many of those who came into contact with her thought that she was not the evil of a psychopathic murderer, but it was the look of fear and devastation of a victim herself.

The background of this child must have had a profound effect on her, she saw regularly things that no child should ever see.

The combination of having only one room in the house and her mother being a prostitute who specialised in Sado Masochism it is believed that she saw everything that went on between her mother and the clients. Many thought this must have influenced Mary, really how could it not?

She would have seen daily physical and sexual violence and sexual attacks between her mother and her clients.

As time passed by Mary's mother Betty became a frequent visitor at Redbank, behind the smiles of the mother and daughter lay an anguished relationship of guilt and resentment.

Betty, the mother received a letter from Mary while she was still at Redbank blaming her for ruining her life

> Please mam put my tiny mind at ease tell judge and jury on your knees they will listen to your cry of plays the guilty one is you not me I'm sorry it has to be this way with both crying and you will go away tell him your guilty please so then mam I'll be free
>
> Your daughter Mary

In 1972, Betty Bell bizarrely gave a television interview, this was still only four years after the killings, she was by then a broken woman relying on drink and drugs to get her through the day.

A transcript of the Television interview

(Interviewer). Are you saying that your daughter is innocent?

(Betty Bell). No, I'm not saying she's innocent

(Interviewer). But something must have made her do these things

(Betty Bell). Yes, something possibly must have made her do these things

(Interviewer). What was it about her life and her family you think that could have driven into these things?

(Betty Bell). Maybe the arguments between my husband and myself had inflect on her, I don't know

(Interviewer). Have you been very despairing sometimes?

(Betty Bell). Very very, a lot of strain, stress and grief for my daughter

The former head of Newcastle Social Services said "*I think the relationship between Mary and her mother was one of the key factors here, where there was little or no emotional attachment at all and I think this made the child feel she had little or no emotional attachment to human beings around her and therefore nasty things could be done to them because it didn't mean anything".*

Child Psychologist Dr Monica Rowbottom, who was involved in the case later said *"So much depends upon what happens to anybody in the first year of their life or two years, you see if they were never exposed to loving attention in those early years they don't learn about love and they don't learn about warmth emotions and so maybe if she had been exposed to loving care from the start things would have been different"*

It was thought that the reason for Mary doing this was that it gave her a sense of power over younger children and that there was some significance to the fact that it was two young boys, but regardless of that, she would not have been able to do that to a person much older because they would have had been too strong for her.

CHAPTER THIRTEEN

FUTURE

Mary Bell spent twelve years locked away, six of them in Redbank secure special unit, the only girl with twenty-two boys.

Whilst there she was occasionally treated by therapists and continued to blame others for the crimes.

September 12th 1977, Mary hit the headlines again at 20 years old she escaped from Moor Court open prison at Stoke-on-Trent, Staffordshire

Inspector Reynolds said that Mary Bell had disappeared from the prison at around tea-time with Annette Priest, a 21-year-old prostitute convicted of stealing from her clients. The two women had been seen by a warder, thumbing a lift in Cheshire.

Mary was returned to prison not long after and was released in 1980 and granted a new identity in 2003.

David Martin a psychologist came to know Mary at Redbank, "*I don't know that she ever*

acknowledged her offences, certainly not to me, not in the slightest, she denied them almost didn't trouble to deny them if you see what I mean it was almost as though you know this just this isn't this isn't the relevant agenda dismissive of them"

Even though she never admitted to the killing of the two boys as she grew up Mary was no longer considered to pose any threat to the community, in 1978
she was moved to Aklam Grange open prison two years later she was released at age 23 there was no public outcry since then she has built a new life with a new name by law her identity is protected from disclosure and by all accounts, it's she's come out of it a very balanced sensible person she sorted out a life with some ups and

downs in it and seemingly thinks she's become a very good citizen now

That shows it can be achieved it can be achieved if time is taken over it and the skills have put him there and there is a real exchange of affection and interest in the person concerned not simply as a case but as a person.

But the people of Scotswood in Newcastle have never overcome the trauma of the case of Mary Bell, the killing of two little boys by an 11-year-old girl seemed to mark a turning point from an old world of comfortable innocence where children could play safely on the streets to a world of high-rise flats increasing crime and an ever-present fear of lurking violence.

Even to this day it's a name that's not forgotten, many things changed, doors are closed children don't play out, and children are taken to school and picked up from school where beforehand they went themselves.

Other cases that have come out have happened since then and they will always be remembered as well, but for some reason because this seems to be the first this will never be forgotten. Twenty-five years after the case of Mary Bell the killing of a toddler by two boys in Liverpool seemed to have many similarities to children egging each other on when they had led off a smaller boy and killed him but the Jamie Bulger case caused much greater public outrage, the video images perhaps had given us a far greater awareness and the violence of the killing seemed more shocking.

Killers Robert Thompson and Jon Venables had a troubled and
unhappy past like Mary, they too
had shown signs of disturbance which were never picked up.
As time passes and we learn more about what causes children to behave in such terrible and extreme ways, one abiding truth emerges is that from birth children must have the loving affection and care of those who look after them.

In a world where such attention can so easily be given, the tragedies which afflicted Newcastle and Liverpool will no doubt come to haunt us again.

Printed in Great Britain
by Amazon